# The Wisdom of Jesus and the Apostles

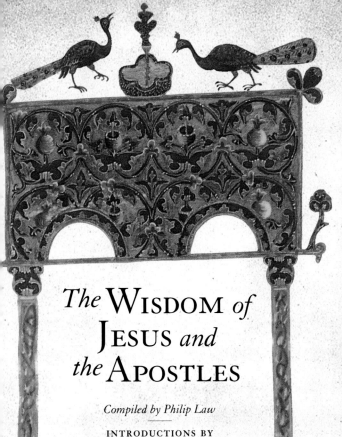

# *The* WISDOM *of* JESUS *and* *the* APOSTLES

*Compiled by Philip Law*

INTRODUCTIONS BY
**Tom Wright and Sister Wendy,**
author of *Sister Wendy's Story of Painting*

GRAMERCY BOOKS
NEW YORK

This 2003 edition is published by Gramercy Books, an imprint of
Random House Value Publishing, a division of Random House, Inc., New York,
by arrangement with Lion Publishing plc, Oxford, England.

Pages 95-96 constitute an extension of this copyright page.

Gramercy is a registered trademark and the colophon is a trademark of
Random House, Inc.

Random House
New York • Toronto • London • Sydney • Auckland
www.randomhouse.com

Printed and bound in China

Library of Congress Cataloging-in-Publication Data

Bible. N.T. Gospels. English. Selections. 2003.
The wisdom of Jesus and the apostles / compiled by Philip Law ;
introductions by Tom Wright and Sister Wendy.
p. cm.
Previously published as 2 vols.: The wisdom of Jesus. c1996
and The wisdom of the apostles. c1997.
ISBN 0-517-22297-3
I. Bible. N.T. Gospels—Quotations. 2. Jesus christ—Teachings. 3. Apostels. 4.
Devotional calendars. I. Law, Philip. II. Bible. N.T. Epistles. English. Selections. 2003.
III. Wisdom of Jesus. IV. Wisdom of the apostles. V. Title.

BS2415.A2L38 2003
225.5'2—dc22

2003049276

10 9 8 7 6 5 4 3 2 1

## CONTENTS

### The Wisdom of Jesus

| | |
|---|---|
| *Introduction* | 9 |
| *Prologue* | 13 |
| *True Wisdom* | 15 |
| *True Happiness* | 21 |
| *True Prayer* | 29 |
| *True Love* | 35 |
| *True God* | 43 |
| *Epilogue* | 49 |

### The Wisdom of the Apostles

| | |
|---|---|
| *Introduction* | 52 |
| *The Wisdom of the Spirit* | 55 |
| *The Grace of God* | 63 |
| *The Meaning of Love* | 71 |
| *The Defeat of Evil* | 79 |
| *The Transformation of the Soul* | 87 |

# *The* WISDOM *of* JESUS

## INTRODUCTION

'No one ever spoke like this man,' said the Temple guards, explaining why they hadn't been able to arrest Jesus. 'They were astonished at his teaching,' wrote one of Jesus' biographers. 'Well said, Teacher,' commented someone who had come to criticize.

What was it that amazed the soldiers, astonished the hearers, and confounded the critics? Read through this book and you'll see. If it's wisdom you're after, this is where to start.

Why is Jesus such an extraordinary teacher? His followers, then and now, regard him as the Son of God. But these teachings are not

9

lofty pronouncements, detached from real life. This is astute wisdom of the highest class.

Hardly surprising, really. It comes out of one of the richest traditions of wisdom in the world. The Jewish Scriptures (which Christians call the Old Testament) are full of poetry, prophecy, and wisdom that cast a clear, healing beam of light on the often murky world of day-to-day living.

Jesus was soaked in these writings, and drew them together in a fresh way.

What's more, Jesus believed that the long story of God and Israel was reaching its climax in his own work. The prophecies would come true: God would teach his people a wisdom that would guide them not simply through this world but on into the new one he was bringing to birth. What you now hold in your hand is a compressed and compelling summary of his message.

Jesus' wisdom, then, isn't just good advice. It's good news. It isn't a set of commands; it's an invitation to open your heart to God's love, to God's call. And with that loving call goes a new strength, a new motivation. Jesus defeated evil. He pioneered a new way of life. This wisdom tells you how you can be part of it.

But there's more. In this wisdom you will find a thumbnail sketch of Jesus himself. His story about a father welcoming a renegade son illustrates and explains his own welcome of outcasts. In the summons to be as wise as a serpent and innocent as a dove we can see a portrait of the speaker.

When he spoke of God's astonishing love, he was also living it out; and, in his death, he acted it out as fully as could be imagined. That's part of what 'Son of God' really means.

Take time, then, over this book. Roll the

phrases around your mouth. Taste their subtle flavour; refresh yourself with the freedom and love they contain.

You might like to learn some of them by heart. You might take a page each day, and think and pray about what it might mean in your life. Above all, you might find yourself coming to recognize the person who stands behind the words. Part of the point of Jesus saying them in the first place was in order to invite people, not just to live by a new wisdom but to share his own love and life.

TOM WRIGHT

*Lichfield Cathedral*
*February 1996*

In the beginning was the Word,
and the Word was with God,
and the Word was God.
He was in the beginning with God.
All things came into being through him,
and without him not one thing came into being.
In him was life,
and the life was the light of all people.
The light shines in the darkness,
and the darkness has not overcome it.
The Word became flesh and lived among us,
and we have seen his glory,
the glory of the Father's only Son,
full of grace and truth.

*John 1:1–5, 14*

# TRUE WISDOM

I

Be wise as serpents
and innocent as doves.

*Matthew 10:16*

## 2
## THE TWO GREAT COMMANDMENTS

A lawyer asked Jesus a question, saying,
'Master, which is the great commandment in the law?'
Jesus said unto him,
' "Thou shalt love the Lord thy God with all thy heart,
and with all thy soul, and with all thy mind."
This is the first and great commandment.
And the second is like unto it,
"Thou shalt love thy neighbour as thyself." '

*Matthew 22:35–39*

# ABANDON YOUR SELF

What good is it for a man to gain the whole world,
yet forfeit his soul?
Or what can a man give in exchange for his soul?

*Mark 8:36–37*

In very truth I tell you,
unless a grain of wheat falls
into the ground and dies,
it remains that and nothing more;
but if it dies, it bears a rich harvest.
Whoever loves himself is lost,
but he who hates himself in this world
will be kept safe for eternal life.

*John 12:24–25*

## 4

# THE SOUL BELONGS TO GOD

Then he told them a parable:
'There was once a rich man who, having had a good harvest from his land, thought to himself, "What am I to do? I have not enough room to store my crops."

'Then he said, "This is what I will do: I will pull down my barns and build bigger ones, and store all my grain and my goods in them, and I will say to my soul: My soul, you have plenty of good things laid by for many years to come; take things easy, eat, drink, have a good time."

'But God said to him, "Fool! This very night the demand will be made for your soul; and this hoard of yours, whose will it be then?"

'So it is when someone stores up treasure for himself instead of becoming rich in the sight of God.'

*Luke 12:16–21*

# BORN OF THE SPIRIT

Now there was a man named Nicodemus, a member of the Jewish ruling council. He came to Jesus at night and said, 'Rabbi, we know you are a teacher who has come from God.' In reply Jesus declared, 'I tell you the truth, no-one can see the kingdom of God unless he is born again.'

'How can a man be born when he is old?' Nicodemus asked. 'Surely he cannot enter a second time into his mother's womb!'

Jesus answered, 'I tell you the truth, no-one can enter the kingdom of God unless he is born of water and the Spirit. Flesh gives birth to flesh, but the Spirit gives birth to spirit. You should not be surprised at my saying, "You must be born again." The wind blows wherever it pleases. You hear its sound, but you cannot tell where it comes from or where it is going. So it is with everyone born of the Spirit.'

*John 3:1–8*

## BECOME LIKE LITTLE CHILDREN

He called a little child and had him stand among them.

And he said: 'I tell you the truth, unless you change and become like little children, you will never enter the kingdom of heaven. Therefore, whoever humbles himself like this child is the greatest in the kingdom of heaven.'

*Matthew 18:2–4*

# TRUE HAPPINESS

---
## 7
---

There is more
happiness in giving
than in receiving.

*Acts 20:35*

# DO NOT BE WORRIED

Do not be worried about the food and drink
you need in order to stay alive,
or about clothes for your body.
After all, isn't life worth more than food?
And isn't the body worth more than clothes?
Look at the birds: they do not sow seeds,
gather a harvest and put it in barns;
yet your Father in heaven takes care of them!

Aren't you worth much more than birds?
Can any of you live a bit longer
by worrying about it?
And why worry about clothes?
Look how the wild flowers grow:
they do not work or make clothes for themselves.
But I tell you that not even King Solomon
with all his wealth had clothes as beautiful
as one of these flowers.

So do not start worrying:
'Where will my food come from?
or my drink? or my clothes?'
Instead, be concerned above everything else with the
Kingdom of God and with what he requires of you,
and he will provide you with all these other things.

Do not worry about tomorrow;
it will have enough worries of its own.
There is no need to add to the troubles each day brings.

*Matthew 6:25–34*

# BE HAPPY!

Happy are those who are spiritually poor;
the Kingdom of heaven belongs to them!
Happy are those who mourn;
God will comfort them!
Happy are those who are humble;
they will receive what God has promised!
Happy are those whose greatest desire is
to do what God requires;
God will satisfy them fully!
Happy are those who are merciful to others;
God will be merciful to them!
Happy are the pure in heart;
they will see God!
Happy are those who work for peace;
God will call them his children!
Happy are those who are persecuted
because they do what God requires;
the Kingdom of heaven belongs to them!

*Matthew 5:3–10*

# HEAVENLY TREASURE

The Kingdom of heaven is like this.
A man happens to find a treasure hidden in a field.
He covers it up again, and is so happy that he goes
and sells everything he has,
and then goes back and buys that field.

*Matthew 13:44*


For where your treasure is,
there will your heart be also.

*Matthew 6:21*

# FIND YOUR TRUE SELF

There was a man who had two sons. The younger of them said to his father, 'Father, give me the share of the property that will belong to me.' So he divided his property between them. A few days later the younger son gathered all he had and travelled to a distant country, and there he squandered his property in dissolute living. When he had spent everything, a severe famine took place throughout that country, and he began to be in need. So he went and hired himself out to one of the citizens of that country, who sent him to his fields to feed the pigs. He would gladly

have filled himself with the pods that the pigs were eating; and no one gave him anything.

But when he came to himself he said, 'How many of my father's hired servants have bread enough and to spare, but here I am dying of hunger! I will get up and go to my father, and I will say to him, "Father, I have sinned against heaven, and before you; I am no longer worthy to be called your son; treat me like one of your hired servants."

So he set off and went to his father. But while he was still far off, his father saw him and was filled with compassion; he ran and put his arms around him and kissed him. Then the son said to him, 'Father, I have sinned against heaven and before you; I am no longer worthy to be called your son.' But the father said to his slaves, 'Quickly, bring out a robe—the best one—and put it on him; put a ring on his finger and sandals on his feet. And get the fatted calf and kill it, and let us eat and celebrate; for this son of mine was dead and is alive again; he was lost and is found!'

*Luke 15:11–24*

# THE JOY OF LOVE

Jesus said to his disciples,
'As the Father has loved me,
so I have loved you;
abide in my love.
If you keep my commandments,
you will abide in my love,
just as I have kept my Father's commandments
and abide in his love.
I have said these things to you
so that my joy may be in you,
and that your joy may be complete.
This is my commandment,
that you love one another as I have loved you.
No one has greater love than this,
to lay down one's life for one's friends.
You are my friends if you do what I command you.
I do not call you servants any longer,
but I have called you my friends,
because I have made known to you
everything that I have heard
from my Father.'

*John 15:9–15*

# TRUE PRAYER

## 13

Whatever you ask for
in prayer,
believe that you have
received it,
and it will be yours.

*Mark 11:24*

# 14

## THE LORD'S PRAYER

This is how you should pray:
Our Father in heaven,
may your name be hallowed;
your kingdom come,
your will be done,
on earth as in heaven.
Give us today our daily bread.
Forgive us the wrong we have done,
as we have forgiven those who have wronged us.
And do not put us to the test,
but save us from the evil one.

*Matthew 6:9–13*

30

# God Hears

Ask, and it will be given to you;
search, and you will find;
knock, and the door will be opened to you.
For everyone who asks receives;
everyone who searches finds;
everyone who knocks will have the door opened.
What father among you,
if his son asked for a fish, would hand him a snake?
Or if he asked for an egg, hand him a scorpion?
If you then, evil as you are,
know how to give your children what is good,
how much more will the heavenly Father
give the Holy Spirit to those who ask him!

*Luke 11:9–13*

## 16

## GOD KNOWS

When you pray, do not be like the hypocrites!
They love to stand up and pray in the houses of worship,
so that everyone will see them.
I assure you, they have already been paid in full.
But when you pray, go to your room, close the door,
and pray to your Father, who is unseen.
And your Father, who sees what you do in private,
will reward you.
When you pray, do not use a lot of meaningless words.
Your Father already knows what you need
before you ask him.

*Matthew 6:5–8*

# GOD IS MERCIFUL

Two men went up to the Temple to pray,
one a Pharisee, the other a tax collector.
The Pharisee stood there
and said this prayer to himself,
'I thank you, God, that I am not grasping, unjust,
adulterous like everyone else,
and particularly that I am not like
this tax collector here.'
The tax collector stood some distance away,
not daring even to raise his eyes to heaven;
but he beat his breast and said,
'God, be merciful to me, a sinner.'
This man, I tell you, went home again justified;
the other did not.
For everyone who raises himself up will be humbled,
but anyone who humbles himself will be raised up.

*Luke 18:10–14*

# THE SPIRIT IS WILLING

They came to a place called Gethsemane, and Jesus said to his disciples, 'The sorrow in my heart is so great that it almost crushes me. Stay here and keep watch.'

He went a little farther on, threw himself on the ground, and prayed that, if possible, he might not have to go through that time of suffering.

'Father,' he prayed, 'my Father! All things are possible for you. Take this cup of suffering away from me. Yet not what I want, but what you want.'

Then he returned and found the disciples asleep. And he said to them, 'Keep watch, and pray that you will not fall into temptation. The spirit is willing, but the flesh is weak.'

*Mark 14:32–38*

# TRUE LOVE

19

Do to others as you
would have them
do to you:
for this is the Law and
the Prophets.

*Matthew 7:12*

# LOVE DOES NOT JUDGE

Do not judge, and you will not be judged.
Do not condemn, and you will not be condemned.
Forgive, and you will be forgiven.
Give, and it will be given to you.
A good measure, pressed down, shaken together
and running over, will be poured into your lap.
For with the measure you use,
it will be measured to you.

Why do you look at the speck of sawdust in your
brother's eye and pay no attention to
the plank in your own eye?
How can you say to your brother, 'Brother, let me
take the speck out of your eye,' when you yourself
fail to see the plank in your own eye?
You hypocrite, first take the plank out of your
eye, and then you will see clearly to remove the
speck from your brother's eye.

*Luke 6:37–38, 41–42*

# LOVE DOES NOT CONDEMN

At daybreak he appeared again in the temple. He had taken his seat and was engaged in teaching, when the scribes and the Pharisees brought in a woman caught committing adultery. Making her stand in the middle, they said to him, 'Teacher, this woman was caught in the very act of adultery. In the law Moses has laid down that such women are to be stoned. What do you say about it?'

Jesus bent down and wrote with his finger on the ground. When they continued to press their question he sat up straight and said, 'Let whichever of you is free from sin throw the first stone.' Then once again he bent down and wrote on the ground. When they heard what he said, one by one they went away, the eldest first; and Jesus was left alone, with the woman still standing there. Jesus again sat up and said to the woman, 'Where are they? Has no one condemned you?' She answered, 'No one sir.' 'Neither do I condemn you,' Jesus said. 'Go; do not sin again.'

*John 8:2–11*

# LOVE DOES NOT LOOK AWAY

On one occasion an expert in the law stood up to test Jesus. 'Teacher,' he asked, 'what must I do to inherit eternal life?'

'What is written in the Law?' he replied.

He answered: ' "Love the Lord your God with all your heart"; and, "Love your neighbour as yourself." '

'You have answered correctly,' Jesus replied. 'Do this and you will live.' But he wanted to justify himself, so he asked Jesus, 'And who is my neighbour?'

In reply Jesus said: 'A man was going down from Jerusalem to Jericho, when he fell into the hands of robbers. They stripped him of his clothes, beat him and went away, leaving him half-dead. A priest happened to be going down the same road, and when he saw the man, he passed by on the other side. So too, a Levite, when he came to the place, passed by on the other side.

But a Samaritan, as he travelled, came where the man was; and when he saw him, he took pity on him. He went to him and bandaged his wounds, pouring on oil and wine. Then he put the man on his own donkey, brought him to an inn and took care of him. The next day he took out two silver coins and gave them to the innkeeper. 'Look after him,' he said, 'and when I return, I will reimburse you for any extra expense you may have.'

'Which of these three do you think was a neighbour to the man who fell into the hands of robbers?'

The expert in the law replied, 'The one who had mercy on him.'

Jesus told him, 'Go and do likewise.'

*Luke 10:25–37*

39

# LOVE DOES NOT EXPECT A REWARD

Love your enemies; do good to those who hate you;
bless those who curse you;
pray for those who treat you spitefully.
If anyone hits you on the cheek, offer the other also;
if anyone takes your coat,
let him have your shirt as well.
If you love only those who love you,
what credit is that to you?
Even sinners love those who love them.
If you do good only to those who do good to you,
what credit is there in that?
Even sinners do as much.
But you must love your enemies and do good,
and lend without expecting any return;
and you will have a rich reward:
you will be sons of the Most High,
because he himself is kind to
the ungrateful and the wicked.
Be compassionate,
as your Father is compassionate.

*Luke 6:27–36*

## 24

# LOVE WILL ALWAYS FORGIVE

When they came to the place that is
called The Skull,
they crucified Jesus with the criminals,
one on his right and one on his left.
Then Jesus said, 'Father, forgive them;
for they do not know what they are doing.'

*Luke 23:33–34*

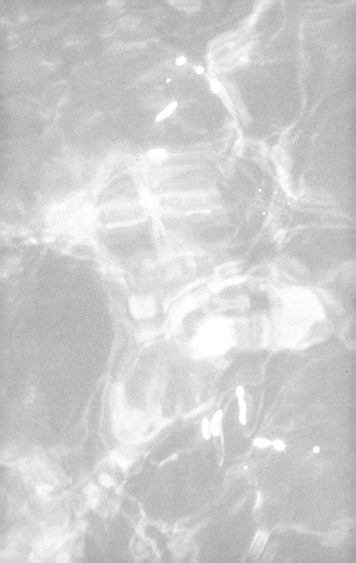

# TRUE
# GOD

---
25

God is spirit,
and those who
worship him
must worship in spirit
and in truth.

*John 4:24*

# THE INVISIBLE KINGDOM

Some Pharisees asked Jesus when the Kingdom
of God would come.

His answer was, 'The Kingdom of God does
not come in such a way as to be seen.

No one will say, "Look, here it is!" or,
"There it is!"; because the Kingdom of God is
within you.'

*Luke 17:20–21*

# THE WAY TO THE FATHER

Jesus said: 'I am the Way; I am Truth and Life.
No one can come to the Father except through me.
If you know me, you will know my Father too.
From this moment you know him and have seen him.'
Philip said, 'Lord, show us the Father
and then we shall be satisfied.'
Jesus said to him, 'Have I been with you all this time,
Philip, and·you still do not know me?
'Anyone who has seen me has seen the Father.'

*John 14:6–10*

# THE SPIRIT WITHIN

I will ask the Father, and he will give you another to be your advocate, who will be with you for ever—the Spirit of truth. The world cannot accept him, because the world neither sees nor knows him; but you know him, because he dwells with you and will be in you. I will not leave you bereft; I am coming back to you.

When that day comes you will know that I am in my Father, and you in me and I in you. Anyone who has received my commands and obeys them—he it is who loves me; and he who loves me will be loved by my Father; and I will love him and disclose myself to him.

*John 14:16–21*

# THE PEACE OF GOD

Peace I leave with you; my peace I give you.
I do not give to you as the world gives.
Do not let your hearts be troubled
and do not be afraid.
The world must learn that I love the Father
and that I do exactly what my Father has
commanded me.

*John 14:27*

I have told you these things, so that in me you
may have peace.
In this world you will have trouble.
But take heart! I have overcome the world.

*John 16:33*

# THE GLORY OF GOD

Then Jesus looked up to heaven and said:
'Father, the hour has come.
Glorify your Son,
that the Son may glorify you.
For you have made him sovereign over all mankind,
to give eternal life to all whom you have given him.
This is eternal life: to know you the only true God,
and Jesus Christ whom you have sent.
I have glorified you on earth by finishing the work
which you gave me to do;
and now, Father, glorify me in your own presence
with the glory which I had with you
before the world began.'

*John 17:1–5*

## EPILOGUE

God so loved the world that he gave his only Son,
that everyone who has faith in him
may not perish but have eternal life.
This is the judgement:
the light has come into the world,
but people preferred darkness to light
because their deeds were evil.
Those who live by the truth come to the light
so that it may be clearly seen that
God is in all they do.

*John 3:16, 19, 21*

# The WISDOM of the APOSTLES

## INTRODUCTION

The apostles really knew Jesus. It was not because they had seen him in action and listened to him. St Paul, for instance, only saw him once, in a dramatic vision, and the gospels show us how very little the followers of Jesus actually understood him. Right to the end, at the last supper itself, we hear Jesus saying sadly to Philip, 'Have I been with you all this time and you still do not know me?' When the arrest came, shortly after, in the Garden of Gethsemane, the apostles revealed their tragic lack of true understanding and all ran away from the Lord. It was only afterwards when Jesus had ascended and sent the Holy Spirit, the spirit of truth, that his disciples at last began to know him. They pondered over what they had seen and heard and had been told by others; they prayed to understand; they held out to him their longing hearts. To this prayer, this desire to know who Jesus is, the Father is never deaf. We can know Jesus just as the apostles did, if that is what we want.

Followers of Jesus come to this blessed knowledge by expressing their need for him in prayer and by reading the Bible. Here, distilled in the words of scripture is the way, the truth and the life — words Jesus used to define what he was and what we can find in him. But the words of scripture are so rich, so dense with holy meaning, so infinite in their levels of revelation that we can easily miss their depths. A little book of extracts is ideal.

We can keep it in our pockets or handbags, have it ready on our desks or bedside tables. We can read a little, let it sink in, marvel at it, live on it. Every word is, in one sense, a judgement: do we show in our daily lives the truth we have read? But it is also a promise: the grace of God will give us these attitudes of love if we set ourselves to desire them. All richness and beauty are here, spread out for us, freely offered. What we have to do is have faith, rest trustingly on the heart of our Father, and long in will for Jesus to be able to praise the Father within us. I say 'in will' because we may not feel this desire: we may only feel the divided anxious mind that St Paul describes so feelingly in extract 19. But he ignored the weak flesh and clung in faith to the spirit of Jesus, and God's grace can empower us to do the same. The 'wisdom of the Apostles' was to know Jesus and to have his mind (see extract 25). Remember what the Lord himself said, 'Ask and you shall receive.'

SISTER WENDY

# THE WISDOM
## OF THE SPIRIT

# A Gift from God

If any of you is lacking in wisdom,
ask God, who gives to all
generously and ungrudgingly,
and it will be given you.

But ask in faith, never doubting,
for the one who doubts is like
a wave of the sea,
driven and tossed by the wind.

*James 1:5–6*

## WISDOM FROM ABOVE

The wisdom that is from above is first pure,
then peaceable, gentle,
and easy to be intreated,
full of mercy and good fruits,
without partiality, and without hypocrisy.

*James 3:17*

# GOD'S FOOLISHNESS

God in his wisdom made it impossible for people to know him by means of their own wisdom. Instead, by means of the so-called 'foolish' message we preach, God decided to save those who believe.

Jews want miracles for proof, and Greeks look for wisdom. As for us, we proclaim the crucified Christ, a message offensive to the Jews and nonsense to the Gentiles; but for those whom God has called, both Jews and Gentiles, this message is Christ, the power of God and the wisdom of God.

For what seems to be God's foolishness is wiser than human wisdom, and what seems to be God's weakness is stronger than human strength.

*1 Corinthians 1:21–25*

## SPIRITUAL DISCERNMENT

We speak of God's secret wisdom, a wisdom
that has been hidden and that God destined
for our glory before time began. As it is
written:

> 'No eye has seen, no ear has heard,
>   no mind has conceived
> what God has prepared for those
>   who love him' –

but God has revealed it to us by his Spirit.
The Spirit searches all things, even the deep
things of God. For who among men knows the
thoughts of a man except the man's spirit
within him? In the same way no-one knows
the thoughts of God except the Spirit of God.

The man without the Spirit does not
accept the things that come from the Spirit of
God, for they are foolishness to him, and he
cannot understand them, because they are
spiritually discerned.

*1 Corinthians 2:7, 9–11, 14*

## 5

## The Practice of Wisdom

Whoever listens to God's word but does not put it into practice is like a man who looks in a mirror and sees himself as he is. He takes a good look at himself and then goes away and at once forgets what he looks like.

But those who look closely into the perfect law that sets people free, who keep on paying attention to it and do not simply listen and then forget it – they will be blessed by God in what they do.

*James 1:23–25*

# THOUGHTS WORTH THINKING

Finally, brothers,
whatever is true, whatever is noble,
whatever is right, whatever is pure,
whatever is lovely, whatever is admirable —
if anything is excellent or praiseworthy —
think about such things.

*Philippians 4:8*

# THE GRACE
## OF GOD

# A LIVING HOPE

Blessed be God the Father of our Lord Jesus
Christ, who in his great mercy has given us
a new birth into a living hope through the
resurrection of Jesus Christ from the dead
and into a heritage that can never be spoilt
or soiled and never fade away. It is reserved
in heaven for you who are being kept safe by
God's power through faith until the salvation
which has been prepared is revealed at the final
point of time.

*1 Peter 1:3–5*

# THE SUPREMACY OF CHRIST

In Christ everything in heaven and on earth was created, not only things visible but also the invisible orders of thrones, sovereignties, authorities, and powers: the whole universe has been created through him and for him.

He exists before all things, and all things are held together in him. He is the head of the body, the church. He is its origin, the first to return from the dead, to become in all things supreme.

For in him God in all his fullness chose to dwell.

*Colossians 1:16–19*

# GOD'S MYSTERIOUS PURPOSE

Blessed be God the Father of our Lord Jesus Christ, who has blessed us with all the spiritual blessings of heaven in Christ. He chose us in Christ before the world was made, to be holy and faultless before him in love. Such is the richness of the grace which he has showered on us in all wisdom and insight.

He has let us know the mystery of his purpose: that he would bring everything together under Christ, as head, everything in the heavens and everything on earth. And it is in him that we have received our heritage, marked out beforehand as we were, under the plan of the One who guides all things as he decides by his own will.

*Ephesians 1:3–4, 7–13*

# GOD'S INDESTRUCTIBLE LOVE

We do not even know how we ought to pray,
but through our inarticulate groans the Spirit
himself is pleading for us, and God who searches
our inmost being knows what the Spirit means,
because he pleads for God's people as God
himself wills; and in everything, as we know, he
co-operates for good with those who love God
and are called according to his purpose.

For those whom God knew before ever
they were, he also ordained to share the
likeness of his Son, so that he might be the
eldest among a large family.

With all this in mind, what are we to say?
If God is on our side, who is against us? I am
convinced that there is nothing in death or life,
in the realm of spirits or superhuman powers,
in the world as it is or the world as it shall be,
in the forces of the universe… nothing in all
creation that can separate us from the love of
God in Christ Jesus our Lord.

*Romans 8:26–31, 38–39*

# GOD'S TRANSCENDENT PEACE

Do not be anxious about anything,
but in everything, by prayer and petition,
with thanksgiving,
present your requests to God.

And the peace of God,
which transcends all understanding,
will guard your hearts and your minds
in Christ Jesus.

*Philippians 4:6–7*

# PARTICIPATION IN GOD

God's divine power has given us everything we need to live a truly religious life through our knowledge of the one who called us to share in his own glory and goodness.

In this way he has given us the very great and precious gifts he promised, so that by means of these gifts you may escape from the destructive lust that is in the world, and may come to share the divine nature.

*2 Peter 1:3–4*

# THE MEANING
## OF LOVE

ΙΩΑΝΝΗΣ Ο ΘΕΟΛΟΓ

71

## TRUE LOVE

If a man say, I love God,
and hateth his brother, he is a liar:
for he that loveth not his brother,
whom he hath seen, how can he love God,
whom he hath not seen?

*1 John 4:20*

Let brotherly love continue.
Be not forgetful to entertain strangers: for
thereby some have entertained angels unawares.

*Hebrews 13:1–2*

## 14

## LOVE'S HARMONY

As God's chosen ones, holy and beloved,
clothe yourselves with compassion, kindness,
humility, meekness, and patience.

Bear with one another and, if anyone has a
complaint against another, forgive each other;
just as the Lord has forgiven you, so you also
must forgive.

Above all, clothe yourselves with love, which
binds everything together in perfect harmony.

*Colossians 3:12–14*


Above all, maintain constant love for one
another, for love covers a multitude of sins.

*1 Peter 4:8*

# GOD'S LOVE WITHIN US

Let us love one another, because the source of love is God.

Everyone who loves is a child of God and knows God. This is how he showed his love among us: he sent his only Son into the world that we might have life through him.

If God thus loved us, my dear friends, we also must love one another. God has never been seen by anyone, but if we love one another, he himself dwells in us; his love is brought to perfection within us.

*1 John 4:7, 9, 11–12*

# THE LOVE OF CHRIST

If then there is any encouragement in Christ,
any consolation from love, any sharing in the
Spirit, any compassion and sympathy… let each
of you look not to your own interests, but to
the interests of others. Let the same mind be
in you that was in Christ Jesus,

who, though he was in the form of God,
did not regard equality with God as
something to be exploited,
but emptied himself,
taking the form of a slave,
being born in human likeness.
And being found in human form,
he humbled himself and became obedient
to the point of death —
even death on a cross.

*Philippians 2:1, 4–8*

# THE GREATEST OF THE VIRTUES

If I speak in the tongues of men and of angels,
but have not love,
I am only a resounding gong
or a clanging cymbal.
If I have the gift of prophecy
and can fathom all mysteries
and all knowledge,
and if I have a faith that can move mountains,
but have not love,
I am nothing.

If I give all I possess to the poor
and surrender my body to the flames,
but have not love,
I gain nothing.
Love is patient, love is kind.
It does not envy, it does not boast,
it is not proud.
It is not rude, it is not self-seeking,
it is not easily angered,
it keeps no record of wrongs.

Love does not delight in evil
but rejoices with the truth.
It always protects, always trusts, always hopes,
always perseveres.
Love never fails.

But where there are prophecies, they will cease;
where there is knowledge, it will pass away.
For we know in part and we prophesy in part;
but when perfection comes,
the imperfect disappears.

When I was a child, I talked like a child,
I thought like a child, I reasoned like a child.
When I became a man,
I put childish ways behind me.
Now we see but a poor reflection
as in a mirror;
then we shall see face to face.
Now I know in part; then I shall know fully,
even as I am fully known.

And now these three remain:
faith, hope and love.
But the greatest of these is love.

*1 Corinthians 13*

# PERFECT LOVE

God is love. Whoever lives in love lives in God, and God in him. In this way, love is made complete among us so that we will have confidence on the day of judgment, because in this world we are like him.

There is no fear in love. But perfect love drives out fear, because fear has to do with punishment. The one who fears is not made perfect in love.

*1 John 4:16–18*

# THE DEFEAT
## OF EVIL

ΙΟΎΔΑϹ

## WHO WILL RESCUE ME?

I know that nothing good dwells in me — my unspiritual self, I mean — for though the will to do good is there, the ability to effect it is not. The good which I want to do, I fail to do; but what I do is the wrong which is against my will; and if what I do is against my will, clearly it is no longer I who am the agent, but sin that has its dwelling in me.

I discover this principle, then: that when I want to do right, only wrong is within my reach. In my inmost self I delight in the law of God, but I perceive in my outward actions a different law, fighting against the law that my mind approves, and making me a prisoner under the law of sin which controls my conduct.

Wretched creature that I am, who is there to rescue me from this state of death?

Who but God? Thanks be to him through Jesus Christ our Lord!

*Romans 7:18–25*

## DRAW NEAR TO GOD

Do you suppose that it is for nothing that the scripture says, 'God yearns jealously for the spirit that he has made to dwell in us'? But he gives all the more grace; therefore it says, 'God opposes the proud, but gives grace to the humble.'

Submit yourselves therefore to God. Resist the devil, and he will flee from you. Draw near to God, and he will draw near to you.

*James 4:5–8*

# THE ROOT OF EVIL

Godliness with contentment is great gain.
For we brought nothing into this world,
and it is certain we can carry nothing out.
And having food and raiment let us be
therewith content.

For the love of money is the root of all
evil: which while some coveted after, they have
erred from the faith, and pierced themselves
through with many sorrows.

*1 Timothy 6:6–8, 10*

# THE HARVEST OF THE SPIRIT

Be guided by the Spirit and you will not gratify the desires of your unspiritual nature. That nature sets its desires against the Spirit, while the Spirit fights against it. They are in conflict with one another so that you cannot do what you want.

But if you are led by the Spirit, you are not subject to law. The harvest of the Spirit is love, joy, peace, patience, kindness, goodness, fidelity, gentleness, and self-control. Against such things there is no law.

Those who belong to Christ Jesus have crucified the old nature with its passions and desires. If the Spirit is the source of our life, let the Spirit also direct its course.

*Galatians 5:16–18, 22–25*

## LOVE ALL THAT IS GOOD

Hate what is evil; cling to what is good.
Be joyful in hope, patient in affliction,
faithful in prayer.
Share with God's people who are in need.
Practise hospitality.
Rejoice with those who rejoice;
mourn with those who mourn.
Live in harmony with one another.
Do not be proud,
but be willing to associate
with people of low position.
Do not repay anyone evil for evil.
If it is possible, as far as it depends on you,
live at peace with everyone.
Do not take revenge, my friends,
but leave room for God's wrath.
Do not be overcome by evil,
but overcome evil with good.

*Romans 12:9, 12–13, 14–19, 21*

# GOD'S WILL FOR YOU

Rejoice always,
pray without ceasing,
give thanks in all circumstances;
for this is the will of God for you.
Do not quench the Spirit.
Do not despise the words of prophets,
but test everything;
hold fast to what is good;
abstain from every form of evil.
May the God of peace sanctify you entirely;
and may your spirit and soul and body
be kept sound and blameless at the coming
of our Lord Jesus Christ.
The one who calls you is faithful,
and he will do this.

*1 Thessalonians 5:16–24*


May mercy, peace and love be yours
in abundance.

*Jude v. 2*

# THE
# TRANSFORMATION
# OF THE SOUL

## DISCERNING GOD'S WILL

Do not model your behaviour on the contemporary world, but let the renewing of your minds transform you, so that you may discern for yourselves what is the will of God – what is good and acceptable and mature.

And through the grace that I have been given, I say this to every one of you: never pride yourself on being better than you really are, but think of yourself dispassionately, recognizing that God has given to each one his measure of faith.

*Romans 12:2–3*

## THE NEW SELF

Get rid of your old self, which made you live
as you used to – the old self that was being
destroyed by its deceitful desires. Your hearts
and minds must be made completely new, and
you must put on the new self, which is created
in God's likeness and reveals itself in the true
life that is upright and holy.

    Do not use harmful words, but only
helpful words, the kind that build up and
provide what is needed, so that what you say
will do good to those who hear you. And do
not make God's Holy Spirit sad; for the
Spirit is God's mark of ownership on you,
a guarantee that the Day will come when
God will set you free.

*Ephesians 4:22–24, 29–30*

## RENEWED IN GOD'S IMAGE

You have been raised to life with Christ, so set your hearts on the things that are in heaven, not on things here on earth. For you have died, and your life is hidden with Christ in God. Your real life is Christ, and when he appears then you too will appear with him and share his glory!

This is the new being which God, its Creator, is constantly renewing in his own image, in order to bring you to a full knowledge of himself.

*Colossians 3:1–4, 10*

## TRANSFORMED BY LIFE

Even though our physical being is gradually decaying, yet our spiritual being is renewed day after day. And this small and temporary trouble we suffer will bring us a tremendous and eternal glory, much greater than the trouble. For we fix our attention, not on things that are seen, but on things that are unseen. What can be seen lasts only for a time, but what cannot be seen lasts for ever.

For we know that when this tent we live in – our body here on earth – is torn down, God will have a house in heaven for us to live in, a home he himself has made, which will last for ever... it is not that we want to get rid of our earthly body, but that we want to have the heavenly one put on over us, so that what is mortal will be transformed by life.

*2 Corinthians 4:16 – 5:1, 4*

# 29
## THE LIBERATION OF CREATION

The created universe is waiting with eager expectation for God's children to be revealed. It was made subject to frustration, not of its own choice but by the will of him who subjected it, yet with the hope that the universe itself is to be freed from the shackles of mortality and is to enter upon the glorious liberty of the children of God.

Up to the present, as we know, the whole created universe in all its parts groans as if in the pangs of childbirth. What is more, we also, to whom the Spirit is given as the firstfruits of the harvest to come, are groaning inwardly while we look forward eagerly to our adoption, our liberation from mortality.

*Romans 8:19–23*

# THE FINAL VICTORY

This is how it will be when the dead are raised to life. When the body is buried, it is mortal; when raised, it will be immortal. When buried, it is ugly and weak; when raised, it will be beautiful and strong. When buried, it is a physical body; when raised, it will be a spiritual body.

Listen to this secret truth: we shall not all die, but when the last trumpet sounds, we shall all be changed in an instant, as quickly as the blinking of an eye. For when the trumpet sounds, the dead will be raised, never to die again, and we shall all be changed... Then the scripture will come true:

'Death is destroyed; victory is complete!'
'Where, Death, is your victory?
Where, Death, is your power to hurt?'

Thanks be to God who gives us the victory through our Lord Jesus Christ!

*1 Corinthians 15:42–44, 51–57*

## Text Acknowledgments

Extracts from the Authorised Version of the Bible (The King James Bible), the rights of which are vested in the Crown, are reproduced by the permission of the Crown's Patentee, Cambridge University Press: pages 11, 26, 36. Scriptures quoted from the Good News Bible, published by the Bible Societies/HarperCollins Publishers Ltd UK © American Bible Society, 1966, 1971, 1976, 1992: pages 12–14, 23, 43–45, 47. Scripture quotations taken from the HOLY BIBLE, NEW INTERNATIONAL VERSION. Copyright © 1973, 1978, 1984 by International Bible Society. Used by permission of Hodder & Stoughton Ltd. All rights reserved: pages 15, 22, 30, 31, 32, 38. New Jerusalem Bible © 1985 by Darton, Longman and Todd Ltd and Doubleday and Company, Inc.: pages 18, 20, 42. Scripture text marked NRSV is from the New Revised Standard Version of the Bible, copyright © 1989 by the Division of Christian Education of the National Council of the Churches of Christ in the USA: pages 10, 27, 29, 35, 39. Revised English Bible © 1989 by permission of Oxford and Cambridge University Presses: pages 19, 21, 28, 34, 37, 46.

## Picture Acknowledgments

1: The Bodleian Library, Oxford, MS E.D. Clarke 10, Byzantine illumination, Gospels c.1100.
2/3, 4, 6, 7, 11, 15, 18, 22, 35, 36, 44 and cover (St James): The Bodleian Library, Oxford, MS Auct. T. inf. 1.10, Byzantine illumination, 'Codex Ebnerianus', Constantinople, early 12th century.
9, 17, 25, 33, 41, 48: The Bodleian Library, Oxford, MS Canon Gr. 110, Byzantine illumination, Acts and Epistles, Constantinople, mid 10th century.

*Series editor:* Philip Law

*Project editor:* Angela Handley

*Book designer:* Nicholas Rous

*Jacket designer:* Gerald Rogers